A Pocket Of Whispers

Lal

/ BookLeaf
Publishing
India | USA | UK

Made with ❤ on the BookLeaf Publishing Platform

www.bookleafpub.in

www.bookleafpub.com

Dedication

You created "Pockets of Love". Dedicated to you and our
one and only Pocket of Love.

Preface

Author's Note

Pocket of Whispers was born from still moments — those fragile spaces between noise and thought, between longing and peace. It is a collection of poems that came to me like soft echoes — reminders that even our smallest feelings, our quietest griefs, and our tenderest joys deserve to be held with care.

Each poem is a pocket — a small vessel of emotion stitched together by words, hope, and reflection. Some pockets hold sorrow, others light. Some hold memories of those we've loved, while others cradle dreams not yet born. Together, they form a tapestry of the human heart — imperfect, resilient, and endlessly kind.

This book is part of my larger journey through Pockets of Love, an initiative rooted in compassion, creativity, and connection. My wish is that these poems reach you as a gentle reminder:
even the softest whisper can heal, and even the smallest pocket can hold an entire universe of love.

— Sharon Joag ☽

Acknowledgements

This book, "Pockets of Love", was born from the simple yet powerful belief that love—shared in small, mindful moments—can bring healing and hope to even the darkest corners of our lives.

To my editor, Sidd Joag, for his thoughtful guidance, patience, and insight throughout this journey.

To my Dad and Mom, whose unwavering love and values have been the foundation of everything I do—thank you for teaching me compassion, resilience, and the beauty of giving, and being a "good person".

To my daughter, Lara. Your light, laughter, and creativity continually inspire me to see the world with open eyes and an open heart.

And to my husband, Anurag—thank you for being my anchor, my encourager, and my greatest source of calm and strength. Your love fills my life with meaning and joy, and I dedicate this work to you and to the quiet, enduring kindness you embody.

Each poem in these pages is a tiny "pocket" of love—

stitched with gratitude, remembrance, and hope for the moments that connect us all.

— Sharon Joag

1. This World Still Beats

A world forgotten
A world unknown
Where the mind unfolds alone
In shadowed corners, softly planned,
Lies the terrace of a phantom land

Silken folds of love once banned,
Whisper secrets hand in hand.
A spirit sharp, nostalgic thrill
Echoes the voice I'm hearing still.

Beyond the mist, where thought stray,
Old dreams rise in pale array.
Time dissolves and shadows blend,
With moments that refuse to end.

A flickering candle, its wavering gleam,
Shows flecks of a lingering dream.
Each dance weaves a veil anew,
Of memories I since outgrew.

Let the phantom winds embrace,
The ruins of this haunted space.
For though forgotten, though unknown,
This world still beats
Within my own.

2. The Ocean Breathes in Waves

With each wave that crashes on shore,
The ocean exhales just once more.
And with all it's might
The ocean breathes in,
Pulling each wave back to it's origin.

I sat on the beach that day,
Where the ocean and sand were at play.
There I watched,
As the ocean brought to land...
Those schools of fish
To dance in the sand.

With each breath the ocean took,
Those clear white fish sought out their nook.
Uncertain if the ocean's sigh
Might cast them on the shore nearby,
Yet, fearful still of venturing far,
They stay close to their schools of Mar.

3. I Want to be Free!

I Want to be Free!

I can't open the door
I can't lift the screen
I just want to come out–
Please, Don't be mean...

I'll keep hiding you see,
Inside my locked house
Please come and Find me
I'm a trembling mouse.

Why can't you find me?
I long to be seen.
Come in and Find me–
I want to be Queen!

They know I'm in here
But no one will tell
Keep this dark secret

Or you'll go straight to Hell

All I can tell you about me,
All that I'll plea:
I'm only a woman-
I want to be Free

I'll be Queen of this Land,
I'll be Queen of the Sun!
Crown me with laughter,
Queen of all Fun!

I can't make a sound
I can't make a peep
Just look all around
I'm buried quite deep.

Over the hedges,
Beyond the old trees,
Come in and find me...
Come, down on your knees.

Dig through the earth,
And you will see-
I've been waiting for someone
For You-
To set me Free!

4. Angels, Their Wings on So High

Angels, Their Wings on so high!
We Stop, and We Watch
As Their Feathers go by...

What are we to do
With Angels so true?
We Watch and We Learn
Until They return.

Where can we find these angels?
In the souls of little girls,
With big long curls?

Or do they live in little boys
While they play with their toys?
These angels we are after-
Are they hiding in our laughter?
Are they so very near
That we don't see them or hear?

There are so many faces..
Am I looking in all the right places?
"Find them Where you least expect," they say-
Are they hiding in my cats as they play?

As I sit and I ponder,
My mind starts to wander..
Oh My! Oh My! Why Couldn't I see?
Haven't you ever thought of this Possibility?

A little whisper in your ear-
That beautiful angel is so near
That voice that says, quite quietly;
"There's an angel hiding inside of ME!"

5. A Kiss of Chardonnay

My senses draw in the waft of an almost sweet, wooden
flavor.
I can barely breathe-
until the cool rim of the glass meets my quivering lips,
waiting for that moment.

The moment when the cold, velvety sweetness
caresses my lips
and engulfs my whole mouth.

The gift of the Gods washes down my throat,
and my eyes close
as warmth rises through my chest-
a burst of golden magic with every sip.

A first kiss with every touch,
a lingering sigh of delight...
A kiss of Chardonnay.

6. That Man

He loved with his Heart
From the very start
He always knew
When I was feeling Blue

If I ever broke a glass
He was never ever crass.
He always said to Me
Loud as could ever be:

"It's just an accident", he'd say,
Smiling gently my way.
Telling me he loved me anyway,
Even if I wasn't his perfect little girl today.

Once late at night
When there was hardly any light
I woke up from my sleep
And found him waiting.

I thought he was waiting...waiting for me
The stars above - a silver sea,
A sea of light that danced so free,
That night still shines inside of me.

I will never forget that gentle stay;
It is in my heart to this very day-
The night we talked till morning's glow,
While the world outside was soft and slow.

I didn't want that night to end,
But now my thoughts I simply send-
Sweet whispers across the way,
To where my Dad is far today.

He lives so far; I cannot see
His smile as often as I'd plea.
But everyday he's in my mind-
A love like his is hard to find.

No day will pass without a prayer,
A thankful thought sent through the air -
For that Man who makes me glad,
Glad that I can call him my Dad.

7. My Bleeding Heart

Inspired by a friend...

My Bleeding Heart in Unable to See
What is standing right in Front of Me.

What can I do
To get through to you?

Can't you see?
I'm in perfect Misery!

But I love you, I do!
Why can't I get through to you?

I want you to go,
Stop knocking at my door.

Please try to feel
My strong arms will create a seal.

How can I trust?
What if this is just lust?

You were hurt in the past..
But we will surely last!

What makes you so sure?
You look so demure.

I know we will last!
Just forget the Past!

My bleeding heart is unable to see
What is standing right in front of me.
How can I start to see
Without a healed heart that can simply BE.

8. Late

I come home so Late
Why is this in my Fate?

I want to be Near,
But my Work is my Fear.

I get on the Train,
And walk in the Rain.

An hour and a Half-
Some think that's a Laugh.

Three hours every day..
What can I say?

Sometimes three becomes four
And she waits- the one I adore.

I want to be there,
I know its not Fair.

What can I do,
To stop feeling Blue?

I am so tired,
When I should be Wired.

I come home to see
My dear, sweet Melody.

We only have one hour to spend,
Before I get a call from a Friend.

And still she waits...
Even if I am very Late.
Why is this in my Fate?

9. Language of the Trees

The Strong Winds you See,
Allow the Branches to Wave
Strangely at Me.
Are they asking me to Play?
Or Just Bidding me "Good Day"?

I wish I could ask this Strange land,
But this is a Tough task to Understand-

The Language of the Trees...
The Secret's in the Breeze

10. The Rock We Eat

The only Rock which we can Eat
Is used to cure all kinds of meat.

Crushed to a Powder
And tossed in Chowder-
It makes our food so bright and sweet,
Even when we are quick to eat!

Can we really eat a Rock?
Oh yes - its quite a Shock!

This rock, you see, is made of salt -
Without it, life would come to a halt.

We always crave just a bit more...
Its only Nature, that's for sure!

11. Why are There People Everywhere?

Inspired by Sonal...

Why am I Here?
Who is that There?
Why are these people Everywhere?

Strange faces- I can't tell.
I Listen for the Voice I Know so Well.
I Breathe in the Air, Searching for her Smell.

Who is that There?
I am Unaware.
All I can do is Squint and Stare.

Why do they throw me
Up in the sky?
Do they really think I can Fly?

Why are there People Every Where?

I need to eat and move my Feet,
So I can feel like I'm complete.

I feel the best
When I am at rest-
Where I belong-
At her chest.

12. Seeds of Tomorrow

God, Please give me the peace to be Free.
To be Free of all this Misery.
When will all of this End?
When will our hearts begin to Mend?

When will I Know?
When I can Sow
The Seeds of Tomorrow-
The Seeds without Sorrow?

13. Darkness

Darkness hides within the Shadows...
Like a Predator, He approaches-
Ready to Pounce upon his Prey.

He creates a Deafening Silence.
From it, No Mortal Can Escape,
Until the Sun Cometh at Dawn...

14. Sweat

As the beads of salt fell from his angry brow,
He charged ahead - bound to one vow.

A vow that he would charge ahead,
Though none could truly comprehend

The fierce voice rising from within,
Compelling him to fight- to win.

How could he ignore his fate,
That led him to this final state?

To regain the love he he's lost before,
He must save his gang once more.

Win he must- this angry War,
So Peace may slowly drift ashore.

And wash away those salty beads,
Leaving only the stillness he so needs.

15. That Little Heart

Do you ever really remark
On that Little Heart waiting after dark?

When Shadows stretch and stars appear,
A little animal knows you're near.
A small ball of fur with eyes so bright,
She waits by the window, night after night.

She pads through halls with tiny feet,
Sniffing the air for your scent so sweet.
Her ears perk up - could that be the car?
She listens closely from afar.

Hour after hour, she guards her space,
Dreaming of your smiling face.
Her heart begins to dance and spark,
When wheels roll home through the dark.

Then - Oh Joy! - the door swings wide!
She wiggles and wags from side to side.

Round and round she twirls and barks,
A song of love that lights the dark.

Do you ever really remark
On that little heart that waits for you
After dark?

16. The Pressure Builds

The Pressure builds;
Inside, it starts to grow -
Could I imagine
Letting all that Pressure go?

What would they think
Sitting right next to me?
Could they connect the link -
The silent blast which set me free?!

17. Bored

There once was a small boy who was always so bored,
No toy or trip they couldn't afford.
Yet still on his face, a frown would stay -
No trace of a smile, no joy in his day.

His parents tried with all their might,
To make him grin or laugh outright.
His mother even cried and cried,
But he just stared, eyes open wide.

Then one bright day he learned to see
Movies that were utterly free.
Not on a screen - but in his head,
From all the books he'd found and read!

Now he smiles from ear to ear,
Adventure waits on every tier!
For the greatest worlds he's ever seen,
Are right inside - his mind's bright screen!

18. Pocket of Love

Every day, she's molding me,
Each day she's growing more.
One day, I will soon be free -
My pocket of love I so adore.

All the while she's searching still,
For the long way home.
The time will come - I know it will -
When she will walk alone.

I can't wait to see her precious face,
And hold her close once more.
Until I must return to that special place,
To touch her hand - forevermore.

www.ingramcontent.com/pod-product-compliance
Lightning Source LLC
Chambersburg PA
CBHW051000030426
42339CB00007B/420